CAMBRIDGE LIBRARY COLLECTION

Books of enduring scholarly value

Archaeology

The discovery of material remains from the recent or the ancient past has always been a source of fascination, but the development of archaeology as an academic discipline which interpreted such finds is relatively recent. It was the work of Winckelmann at Pompeii in the 1760s which first revealed the potential of systematic excavation to scholars and the wider public. Pioneering figures of the nineteenth century such as Schliemann, Layard and Petrie transformed archaeology from a search for ancient artifacts, by means as crude as using gunpowder to break into a tomb, to a science which drew from a wide range of disciplines - ancient languages and literature, geology, chemistry, social history - to increase our understanding of human life and society in the remote past.

The Xanthian Marbles

The traveller and archaeologist Sir Charles Fellows (1799–1860) made several trips through Asia Minor. His careful observations of ancient cities that were at that time unknown to Europeans captured the attention of readers of his published journals and fuelled the British Museum's desire to acquire antiquities from the region. This brief work, first published in 1843, seeks to explain and justify how Fellows shipped dozens of cases of sculptures and architectural remains to Malta from Xanthos, an important city in ancient Lycia. It includes correspondence relating to the practicalities of carrying out the expedition and securing permission to do so from the Ottoman authorities. Fellows was later knighted for his role in these acquisitions, though controversy surrounds their removal. His well-illustrated accounts of his two previous trips to Asia Minor are also reissued in this series.

T0352291

Cambridge University Press has long been a pioneer in the reissuing of out-of-print titles from its own backlist, producing digital reprints of books that are still sought after by scholars and students but could not be reprinted economically using traditional technology. The Cambridge Library Collection extends this activity to a wider range of books which are still of importance to researchers and professionals, either for the source material they contain, or as landmarks in the history of their academic discipline.

Drawing from the world-renowned collections in the Cambridge University Library and other partner libraries, and guided by the advice of experts in each subject area, Cambridge University Press is using state-of-the-art scanning machines in its own Printing House to capture the content of each book selected for inclusion. The files are processed to give a consistently clear, crisp image, and the books finished to the high quality standard for which the Press is recognised around the world. The latest print-on-demand technology ensures that the books will remain available indefinitely, and that orders for single or multiple copies can quickly be supplied.

The Cambridge Library Collection brings back to life books of enduring scholarly value (including out-of-copyright works originally issued by other publishers) across a wide range of disciplines in the humanities and social sciences and in science and technology.

The Xanthian Marbles

Their Acquisition,
and Transmission to England

CHARLES FELLOWS

CAMBRIDGE
UNIVERSITY PRESS

University Printing House, Cambridge, CB2 8BS, United Kingdom

Cambridge University Press is part of the University of Cambridge.

It furthers the University's mission by disseminating knowledge in the pursuit of
education, learning and research at the highest international levels of excellence.

www.cambridge.org
Information on this title: www.cambridge.org/9781108080675

This edition first published 1843
This digitally printed version 2015

ISBN 978-1-108-08067-5 Paperback

THE

XANTHIAN MARBLES;

THEIR

ACQUISITION, AND TRANSMISSION

TO

ENGLAND.

LONDON:

JOHN MURRAY, ALBEMARLE STREET.

MDCCCXLIII.

PRINTED BY RICHARD AND JOHN E. TAYLOR,
RED LION COURT, FLEET STREET.

THE manuscript of the following pages was prepared as a register of the incidents connected with the acquisition of the Xanthian marbles by the British Museum ; and, had not circumstances induced its publication, would have been deposited among the records in that institution.

Finding that vague rumours, imperfect accounts and misrepresentations were appearing in the public prints, I have thought fit, notwithstanding the necessarily egotistical character of the narrative, to give it publicity in its original form, and therefore preface the account with this apology.

CHARLES FELLOWS.

London, December 14, 1842.

A view of part of the ruins of
XANTHUS
Shewing the sites whence the marbles
were taken :—

Pubᵈ by Ionn Murray, London

Charles Fellows 1842

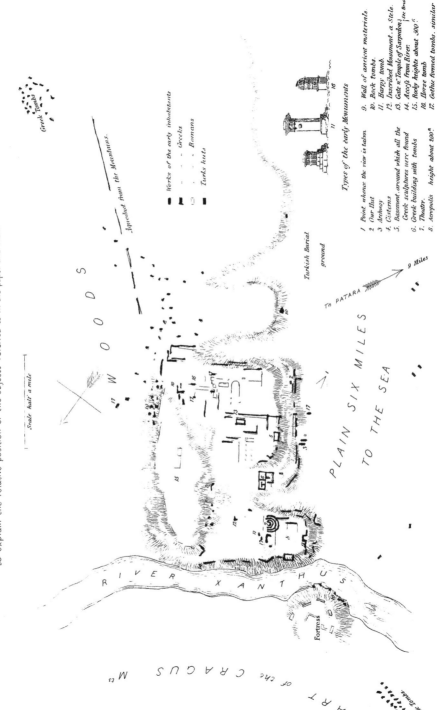

MAP OF XANTHUS

to explain the relative position of the objects referred to in the paper and view.

— Scale half a mile

Aqueduct from the Mountains.

W O O D S

Greek Tombs

PART of the CRACUS M.ⁿˢ

R I V E R   X A N T H U S

Fortress

P L A I N   S I X   M I L E S
T O   T H E   S E A

To PATARA   9 Miles

Turkish Burial ground

Works of the early inhabitants
  ■   Greeks
  ▫   Romans
  ▪   Turks huts

Types of the early Monuments.

1 Point whence the view is taken.
2 Our Hut
3 Archway
4 Cisterns
5 Basement around which all the Greek sculptures were found
6 Greek building with tombs
7 Theatre.
8 Acropolis   height about 200.ᶠᵗ

9   Wall of ancient materials
10 Rock tombs.
11 Harpy tomb.
12 Inscribed Monument. a Stele.
13 Gate n.ᵒ Temple of Sarpedon. } see Bruhn
14 Access from River.
15 Rocky heights about 500.ᶠᵗ
16 Horse tomb.
17 Gothic formed tombs. similar

THE

XANTHIAN MARBLES.

DURING my travels in Asia Minor in the spring of
1838, I was so much struck by the beauty and pecu-
liarity of the architectural remains on the coast of the
province of Lycia, that I determined, if possible, to
penetrate into the interior of the country.

Observing from the works of Colonel Leake and
others that the valley of the Xanthus would probably
be found to contain ancient cities, and that it had never
yet been explored, I commenced my researches at Patara, and within a few miles up the valley discovered the
extensive and highly interesting ruins of Xanthus, the
former capital of Lycia. I afterwards found another
large city, whose situation alone would point it out as
the most beautiful of ancient sites: this by inscriptions
I found to be the city of Tlos: other piles of ruins I saw
and heard of in the mountains, but I was unprepared to
remain longer in the country.

On my return to England, the publication of my
Journal, and my numerous drawings and inscriptions,

attracted the attention of some of the leading men*
connected with the British Museum, and they in the
spring of 1839, at my urgent request, applied to Lord
Palmerston to ask of the Sultan a firman or letter,
granting leave to bring away some of the works of ancient art which I had discovered.

In the autumn of 1839, finding that I could gain no
information from books of the interesting district which
I had visited, I again left England for Lycia, more fully
prepared for a re-examination of its geography and works
of art.   To secure an accurate representation of the latter, I took with me Mr. George Scharf, a young English
artist.   Anticipating the possession of the firman from
the Sultan, I offered to the Trustees of the British Museum my personal services while in Lycia, in pointing out
the most desirable objects to remove.   From Smyrna I
wrote to Lord Ponsonby, our ambassador at Constantinople, to urge the importance of obtaining the firman by
the spring of 1840, and requesting that it might be forwarded to the ship, ordered by the Government to be at
Rhodes on the 1st of May. On the 12th of May I found
at Rhodes the following letter from Lord Ponsonby :—

" Sir,   " *March* 7, 1840.
" I have had the honour to receive your letter of the 23rd of
February, and immediately made application to the Sublime

---

* To the well-directed zeal of Mr. Hawkins, furthered by two of the
Trustees, the Marquis of Northampton and Mr. Hamilton, the country
is indebted for the promotion of this expedition.

Porte for a firman, such as you desire to have, but I regret to say the Porte objects to the extent and to the *generality* of the demand, and I am much afraid I shall not be able to obtain what you want: I will do all in my power. There are other obstacles, besides what I have mentioned, of a nature that I cannot explain to you. Should I succeed, I will send the firman to Smyrna, to Her Majesty's Consul. I have no means of sending it to you.

> " I have the honour to be, Sir,
>> " Your most obedient, humble servant,
>>> " PONSONBY."

At this period I had discovered thirteen other cities in Lycia, and each containing works of ancient art. Returning to England, I again laid before the public my Journal, and with increased zeal the Government applied to Lord Ponsonby; but it was not until October 1841 that the Trustees of the Museum received information that the firman was at last obtained, and was left in the hands of the Consul at Smyrna, at the same time urging the necessity of its being promptly acted upon, and stating the difficulties experienced in obtaining the document.

I was applied to by the Museum to furnish forthwith full instructions as to what objects were to be removed, and to make maps, plans, and descriptions as to where each fragment was to be sought by the Captain of such of Her Majesty's ships as might be appointed to the service. I felt certain that the removal of one stone would bring to light others, probably better preserved and more valuable, and that the *visible* formed but a fraction of what might be obtained, but could not be enumerated in written orders, which might probably be only literally obeyed. With these feelings I wrote the following letter to the Secretary of the British Museum :—

    " Dear Sir,   "*October* 12, 1841.

    " At the request of the Trustees of the Museum, I furnish written instructions for the finding the monuments about to be removed from Lycia. I feel that, should this expedition fail in any point, it will be from a want of local knowledge of the country and manners of the people; and as my interest in the works of art makes me feel almost responsible for their safety into our care, I write to offer my services to point out the objects for removal. There is little pleasurable in wintering in a tent, or in a sea-voyage at this season to a spot I have already twice visited; but I should hereafter regret any incompleteness in the expedition which I could have prevented. Of course I require no remuneration, and I pay my own expenses, but shall expect a free passage out and home in some of Her Majesty's packets, and rations with the officers. Should this meet the approbation of the Trustees, perhaps you will be kind enough to let me know.

    " Believe me to remain, yours very truly,

                         " CHARLES FELLOWS."

" To the Rev. J. Forshall,
Secretary, British Museum."

In reply I received a letter, dated the 15th of October, accepting my proffered services, and stating that the papers were made up for the vessel starting on the 17th, and showing the necessity of my accompanying them in order to secure a passage from Malta in the ship appointed to the expedition, which would probably sail on the arrival of the dispatches. The reply concludes, " The Trustees are very sensible of the liberality and public spirit which your proposal to them manifests, and do not doubt that the naval officer employed on the service will derive essential advantage from your presence and counsel."

The dispatches and all the requisites for the expedition were therefore made up independently of my accompanying it, which was solely for the purpose of pointing out to the Captain the objects to be removed. On the 16th of October, within thirty-six hours from the receipt of this letter, I was on board the Tagus steam-packet off Southampton, with my tent, canteen, bedding and stores, supplied with no other authority than an order to be received on board Her Majesty's ship, about to sail from Malta for Xanthus.

On my arrival at Malta on the 30th of October, I found that Captain Graves, of Her Majesty's ship Beacon, then off the Island of Paros, had been selected for the service ; and the Admiral commanding in chief at once ordered the Vesuvius steam-ship to take me, together with three months' additional stores for the Beacon, to join the ship. On the 8th of November we arrived at Port Naussa, where the surveying-ship was anchored. A delay of a week here occurred in collecting the small vessels which were out surveying along the coasts. The Isabella, a schooner with Mr. Hoskyn, the master of the Beacon, was then in Lycia, where he had spent most of the summer in examining and mapping the valley of the Xanthus. On board the Beacon I saw plans of the ruins of the city of Xanthus, as well as maps of the valley, the result of his labours during the previous winter.

On witnessing the opening of the dispatches to Captain Graves, I was surprised to find that no funds were provided for the expedition, nor was the subject at all referred to in any of the papers. The orders to the Captain were simply to this effect : " To sail to Smyrna for the firman, and thence to the nearest safe anchorage to the mouth of the river Xanthus, and there to put on board and bring away to Malta such objects as should be pointed out by Mr. Fellows." This omission of placing funds in the hands of the Captain of the expedition was the first impediment I encountered ; but knowing that the necessary expenses would be small, being merely for tools, trifling presents to the peasantry, or the occasional hire of their cattle, I offered to provide the funds required, feeling sure that the Trustees of the Museum had inadvertently omitted the supplies, but would gladly repay any sums advanced.

We arrived at Smyrna on the 15th of November : a heavier cloud here hung over the expedition. The documents left with the Consul, and represented in an accompanying letter from our Ambassador to him, as well as to the Government at home, as "the necessary firman," and on which representation I had left England, were found to be only letters dated long before, and proposing that inquiry should be made as to what was desired by England, and to wait a report from the local authorities as to the practicability of granting the request. I give a copy of the papers.

Translation of a letter from His Excellency the Grand Vizir to the Muhassil, to the Judge, and to the Effendis and Agas composing the Municipal Council of the Sangiak of Menteché.

" It is known to the British Government that there are some stones sculptured with art, built into some walls at a place near Eksekuid, a village in the dependency of Macri, in the Sangiak of Menteché, and into the walls of the fortress of Boudroum ; and as these stones are antique remains and rare objects, His Excellency the English Ambassador has demanded and solicited by a memorial that they might be removed from thence, and be given as a present to the British Government.

" Although it is necessary, in consideration of the friendship that exists between the Sublime Porte and the Court of Great Britain, to accede to such demands, yet it has been judged expedient first of all to take some information respecting the stones in question.

" You will begin, therefore, by informing us, without delay, what it would be necessary to do in order to take away these stones, and replace them by others ; and it is for this reason that I have written and sent this letter to you.

" The 17th Rébud Ahker, 1257; corresponding with 7th June, 1841.

" L.
Riouf
S."

The above was accompanied by a letter from the Dragoman of the British Embassy, of which the following is a Copy :—

" My Lord,   " *Pera, June* 10, 1841.

" In transmitting to your Excellency His Highness the Grand Vizir's letter concerning the sculptures of Xanthus and Halycarnassus, I am happy to inform you that I have Rifaat Pasha's word that they will be given to Her Majesty's Government. His Excellency tells me that the letter, such as it is, has been thought necessary as a first step.

" I beg leave strongly to recommend a measure which I consider as being indispensable : it is, that the vizirial letter should be presented to the authorities of Menteché by some person capable to point out the stones therein alluded to. Everybody knows that the modern name of Halycarnassus is Boudroum; but who can say exactly the present Turkish name for Xanthus ? From what I know, Xanthus must be at, or very near, the village of Eksekuid, and the letter has been written in consequence.

" In order, therefore, to leave no pretext for the authorities to make difficulties, and say that they do not exactly know where the stones are, some well-informed person must go to the very spot.

" Some well-qualified person might be found at Smyrna : Xanthus is, at all events, in the Sangiak of Menteché.

" I have the honour to be, with the greatest respect,
" My Lord,
" Your Excellency's most obedient, humble servant,
" FREDERICK PISANI."

" *To His Excellency Viscount Ponsonby,*
&c. &c. &c."

The expedition must here have failed, as Captain Graves could only return and report to the Admiral, who would communicate with England, and an application to the Porte must have followed; and in the slowness of diplomatic proceedings, this might be months or years in coming to maturity. My official friends around me at Smyrna entertained but little hope of our overcoming the difficulties which faced us; but I saw a ray of light, and decided on the course to pursue. My anticipated duty was simply to point out the objects to be removed. It was now necessary to assume the management of obtaining the proper authorities, which did not come within the duty of the Captain. My mission extended only to the removal of the marbles from *Xanthus*, and the orders from the Admiral were also limited to that duty.

I observed that Lord Ponsonby had included in his request permission to remove marbles now built into the inner walls of one of the principal fortresses of the Sultan, the castle at Boodroom, the ancient Halicarnassus. The application to Lord Ponsonby to request this of the Sultan was made more than two years after his application for the Xanthian Marbles, and I had no instructions respecting them; nor would I have been a party to ask what, to all who have seen them, must be considered an unreasonable request. I felt sure that, if properly explained, no objection could be made to the removal of the buried stones in the almost unknown mountains of Lycia. I therefore resolved to go to Constantinople and ask for these only, and, if I failed, then to return to England. To assume an appearance of authority, of which I had but little in reality, I requested Captain Graves to accompany me in the steam-packet, leaving his ship at Smyrna. We arrived on the 21st of November, and on the first application to the authorities* I was gratified in finding that I had judged rightly. Riouf Pasha observed, that he was glad that the other part of the request was withdrawn, as he feared it never could have been granted; that no difficulty now remained, and a firman should be given forthwith for the marbles from Xanthus. Captain Graves returned to Smyrna immediately, and I awaited the tedious progress of state papers until the 30th, when I received the necessary document from the Dragoman, while on board the vessel in which I was starting for Smyrna. In the whole transaction with the officers of state in obtaining this authority, the greatest attention was paid, and not the slightest fee was expected or given.

The following is a translation of the Authority :—

A letter from H.H. the Grand Vizir to Hadgi Ali Pasha, Governor of Rhodes, dated the 15th of Sheoval, 1257 (the 29th of November, 1841).

After the usual titles.

" The British Embassy has represented by a *tairer* [a note in Turkish], that there are some antiques consisting in sculptured

---

* I am indebted to Mr. Bankhead, the Minister Plenipotentiary, for his attention to my wishes in communicating with the authorities.

stones, lying down, and of no use, at a place near the village of *Koonik*, in the District of Marmoriss, which is one of the dependencies of Rhodes, and not far from the sea-shore ; and has requested that the antiques aforesaid should be given to the British Government, for the purpose of putting them in the Museum.   The British Embassy has in the meantime represented, that the distinguished Captain Graves has been ordered by the British Government to embark those stones and to carry them to England ; and that as he is going himself to the spot a letter was asked in his behalf, that your Excellency may give him every assistance on this occasion.

" The Sublime Porte is interested in granting such demands, in consequence of the sincere friendship existing between the two Governments.   If, therefore, the antiquities above mentioned are lying down here and there, and are of no use, Your Excellency shall make no objection to the Captain's taking them away and carrying them on board ; and to that effect you will be pleased to appoint one or two of your attendants to accompany him.   Should any great obstacle exist in giving them, you will write him on the subject, that we may do what is necessary.

" Such are the Sultan's commands, in conformity to which you will act ; and, consequently, I write and forward to Your Excellency the present dispatch.

" L.

Mehemed

Riouf

S."

The knowledge of the boundaries of the various Pashalics of the remote districts is very limited at Constantinople.   I therefore myself gave instruction for the letter, and although imperfect I could then obtain no better authority. On my return to Smyrna I learned more, and, fearing verbal irregularity, I provided a present for the Pasha, to whom it was addressed*.

After purchasing spades, pickaxes, crowbars, and all that was considered essential, we sailed on the 2nd of

---

* In order to show the power exercised on the letter of the law by Turkish authorities,—and sometimes, no doubt, they are instructed so to act, rather than that the head authority should at once refuse the request,—I add some anecdotes which may also show the extreme jealousy the Turks have of their fortresses being visited by Franks.

Some English travellers being anxious to examine the sculpture represented to be built within the walls of the castle of Boodroom, and knowing the difficulty in gaining admittance, took the precaution to obtain an order from Constantinople to go "round the fortification at Boodroom." The governor of the castle received the order with every mark of respect, and offered the usual hospitality of the East; after which he told the travellers, that the mandate could not admit them *within* the castle, as his orders were most strict on that point, but they might go "round the fortification."

This was a joke against the English travellers: some French gentlemen profited by the warning, and were more particular in having their authority worded, desiring that they might "go within and examine anything they required." The same respect was shown to them by the governor; but as they entered, he called their attention to one point in the order, observing that he had no power to let them out of the castle again. I need not add the effect of this intimation.

The Rev. V. Arundell also obtained leave to "take down" some sculpture from a gateway at Ephesus, which he accomplished with difficulty : here the Aga interposed, stating that the authority did not extend to taking the stones away. They were consequently left, and afterwards, in the course of time, destroyed.

December for Rhodes. Thirty hours is the usual passage for the Austrian steam-vessels; we were sixteen days at sea,—arriving at Rhodes on the 18th of December. As our mission was to the Pasha from the Sultan, we thought it advisable, more particularly as there were several weak points in the wording of the letter, to pay to the Pasha every mark of respect. The Captain, therefore, sent to know what salute he would allow, on which he requested seventeen guns at 8 o'clock on the following morning, which were answered by as many from the old castle over our heads. The Captain, three of his officers, and myself, accompanied by our Consul, had an audience at 9 o'clock, when we were received with every mark of attention. Our letter was read aloud to the Pasha, and much conversation followed between him and his secretary. This arose upon points of difficulty, all of which were surmounted by the will and kindness of the Pasha. The river Xanthus, which flows at the foot of the Acropolis of the ancient city, is the boundary of the Pashalic; the ruins, the scene of our intended operations, lay beyond, on the southern banks of the river, and therefore within the Pashalic of Adalia; but it was decided that we should proceed with our expedition on the responsibility of the Pasha of Rhodes, and in the meantime the documents should be forwarded to the Aga at Fornas, the nearest authority to the ruins, and he was to send a messenger with them to Adalia; our Pasha observing, "that the instructions were the same to whomsoever they might be addressed*." Two excellent men, the chiefs of the Police (Cavasses), were appointed to accompany us, perhaps in the double capacity of a guard of honour, and to see justice done between all parties; they were to protect us from imposition, and to report any oppression of the peasantry by us.

We sailed from Rhodes, but forty-five miles from our destination, on the 21st of December, and did not arrive until the 26th: our voyages were most tedious.

The Captain could not find a secure berth for the ship in Kalamaky Bay: he therefore landed some stores and the men for the expedition, and sailed for the Bay of Macry, about fifty miles to the northward, where also lay the Isabella with Mr. Hoskyn. My surprise was great on hearing from the Captain, a few hours before we were put on shore, that neither he nor any of his surveying officers were to be of the expedition, and that the whole was to be left to his first Lieutenant, who was a stranger to the country and had recently joined the ship. I urged the necessity for all the engineering skill the Captain could spare, to which he replied, that they could not leave the charts, but perhaps he might come down to see us. I was landed with the first party in order to seek the

* After we had been some weeks at work in the ruins, our acts were confirmed by a message from the Pasha of Adalia, saying, that " the Queen of England was good, the Sultan was good, and that we were all brothers, and that we might take what we liked."

mouth of the river, which was not laid down in the charts. After a walk of two or three miles we found it, and made signals for the other boats. The party landed consisted of fifteen working-men, a boy, the Lieutenant, the Gunner, the Cavasses, a youth, the son of Mr. Wilkinson, our Consul at Rhodes, and myself. Our five tents were soon pitched, fires lighted, and our cutter, galley, and dingy boats secured within the river. High sand-hills arose for miles around us, and no signs of life were visible but the footsteps of the wolves, jackals, and hares. Huge trunks of decayed trees, washed down during past ages, afforded plenty of fuel for our fires, which vied with the full moon in illuminating our encampment, and must have served as a beacon to our ship, which had sailed afar to the northward.

The river Xanthus is one of the most powerful, wild, and unmanageable streams I ever saw : the volume of water is very great, far exceeding that of the Thames at Richmond ; the stream rushes probably at the rate of five miles an hour. For the first three miles from its mouth, where it winds through the high range of sand-hills, I had never before seen it, but above this had traced it to its source in the Yeeilassies of the high mountains of the Taurus, probably a course of nearly two hundred miles. Our boats drew two feet and a half of water, and had great difficulty in making head against the heaviest part of the stream, which marked the deepest channel through the bar of sand formed at the entrance to the river. Once within this, to accomplish which cost

us much labour and risk, the men having to jump over-
board to keep the boats in their course, the waters were
deep and comparatively tranquil.

In manning our boats on the morning of the 27th we
found that the eight oars in the cutter made no way
against the stream ; we therefore abandoned them, and
set all hands to work in tracking the lightened boats
with ropes from the shore, leaving in them only a cock-
swain and one man, who with a pole had continually to
fathom the water ahead. From the gulfy nature of the
river the depth often varied, within the length of the
boat, from fifteen to two feet, and in the turbid waters
these shoals could be avoided only by keeping in the
strongest streams ; the labour was therefore great ; axes
and billhooks were in constant use, in cutting away the
branches of trees overhanging the river, which inter-
rupted the towing-line. For this labour we soon found
our men insufficient to work the two boats ; we therefore put all hands to one, and at noon pitched the tents
and returned to bring the other boat to our place of
halting, which was within the range of sand-hills, and
on the plain extending to the ruins of the ancient city
of Xanthus. This flat is apparently covered with un-
derwood of myrtle, oleander, storax, and tamarisk, but
is occasionally cleared for patches of cultivation. Our
encampment soon attracted the attention of the pea-
sants, whose invisible tents and huts were sheltered
with their flocks amongst the bushes : their astonish-
ment at everything they saw was evinced by groups

collected on every hillock around us ; and I soon found that the hospitality and kindness which I had before experienced was with this people a custom: eggs, poultry, fruit and milk were brought to us, and every attention afforded ; they acted as pilots, by wading over the shallows and pointing out our best course for the boats. Four days were we navigating our little stores up the river to the ancient city, a course not exceeding nine miles, and which we afterwards commonly ran down in a boat within three quarters of an hour.

Our early halts each day gave me leisure for little rambles, and within a mile of our first encampment I visited some ancient walls, which on my former tours were inaccessible on account of the swamps surrounding them. I was much pleased at finding a beautiful little theatre, with its back within an isolated rocky hill ; over the door was a series of grotesque masks, perhaps representing the passions ; there was no trace of the proscenium, and I was again induced to believe that this part of the ancient theatres might have been sometimes constructed of wood and destroyed by time. Near the theatre were the ruins of a building, probably a small temple, which had been ornamented by columns. No former city was to be traced, and I have little doubt that this was the sacred grove and haunt of Latona, the Letoum which in my last Journal I suggested was on this spot.

Our evenings were not without amusement ; the sailors soon made bats and balls, and cricket was perhaps for the first time played in Lycia ; at all events the wonder expressed by the living generation showed that it was not a game known to the present inhabitants. The weather was delightful ; the thermometer at night at 40°, and in the day 64°. Our nights, which were lighted by a full moon, were often varied by alarm of wild beasts, or rather a hope that we might have some sport ; the gunner distributed arms to the men, but the game was too wary for inexperienced sportsmen ; when we were still, the wild boars and their young came grunting past our tents, and the wolves and jackals howled around us, but the slightest movement among our men only caused the flight of wild ducks, and all was still again.

On the 30th of December we pitched our tents on the plain immediately beneath the ruins of the ancient city. During the three following days rain fell almost incessantly and we could do little but protect our tents from the effect of the falling torrents by cutting drains around our encampment. We cleared away the brushwood from the scenes of our future labours, and busily contrived abodes for the men, less pervious to the elements and upon higher ground. We reconstructed the ruined walls of a barn, and with fresh-cut trees* formed rafters which were wattled with brushwood : over this were

* We had permission to cut down any trees excepting the Velanéa oak (*Quercus Ægylops*) ; the acorn of this produces a revenue to the Sultan

thrown sail-cloths, and a good barrack formed for double our number of men. The gunner's tent and one for the tools were pitched by the side. For the officers and myself, I induced a family, consisting of a mother, two daughters, and a son, to leave us their hut, which was admirably situated for our works. I found, as on my former visits to these people, that money was not the powerful inducement; all offers were ineffectual to persuade them to remove, until we represented the extreme damp and inconvenience we felt from the low ground and from remaining in our tents. They then agreed to move their family to about half a mile distant, and we whitewashed and entered our picturesque abode on the 2nd of January*. Half our hands had gone down to the coast to bring up a part of the stores of planks, poles, ropes, &c., which we had been obliged to leave behind, and with the four or five remaining working men we could do but little in commencing our operations.

The object of the expedition was the bringing away the bas-reliefs representing the legend of the Daughters of King Pandarus, which were around a *stele*, or high square monument, which we called the "Harpy Tomb,"—the beautiful gothic-shaped tomb having chariots and horses

* Our room was twelve feet square; upon the floor of this we occasionally spread eleven beds : the servants occupied the portico, which also served as our kitchen. The Cavasses had a hut to themselves, which was the resort of all the passing Turks; in the evening they had often music, and sometimes a dance—amusements similar to those described in my "Lycia."

sculptured upon its top, which we called the "Horse Tomb," and some three or four fragments of sculpture built into walls. These were the specified visible objects we sought to remove; but I expected to find much more, and I was not mistaken.

I had noticed in my Journal that, from the massive foundation still built-in with its rock upon the brow of a cliff immediately above our tents, in all probability temples had stood; two fragments of sculptured frieze which I had noticed among the bushes strengthened this opinion : of these I have given engravings in my "Lycia." I determined to seek here for more ; and on the 7th and 8th of January, with my five men, found in a few hours two other portions of friezes near the same spot. Down the precipice in front of this site lay an avalanche of stones and piles on either side along the edge of the cliffs. These stones differed in size, but might average a ton each ; the upper ones, which had last fallen, and had formed the base of the building above, weighed many of them seven or eight tons each, but from their position on the side of the hill they were not difficult to remove.

The 9th of January was Sunday, when all the men after service generally rambled about, and it often happened that it was the most prolific day for discoveries. In endeavouring to catch a scorpion, I crept into a hole among a pile of large blocks of white marble, and to my great joy saw above me, upon the under side of a stone, an Amazon on horseback, and a fine naked figure with a shield, the whole as white and perfect as when first sculptured. Within an hour, with the aid of some of the men, we found sufficient work for the following week, and anxiously did I await the Monday morning, the first mustering of our full complement of men. Five more stones were brought to light on the 10th.

The Harpy Tomb consisted of a square shaft in one block, weighing about eighty tons, its height seventeen feet, placed upon a base rising on one side six feet from the ground, on the other but little above the present level of the earth. Around the sides of the top of the shaft were ranged the bas-reliefs in white marble, about three feet three inches high; upon these rested a capstone, apparently a series of stones, one projecting over the other; but these are cut in one block, probably fifteen to twenty tons in weight. Within the top of the shaft was hollowed out a chamber, which, with the bas-relief sides, was seven feet six inches high, and seven feet square. This singular chamber had been probably in the early ages of Christianity the cell of an anchoret, perhaps a disciple of Simeon Stylites, whose name he derived from his habitation, which I believe we have generally translated as meaning a column, but the form now in question is undoubtedly a *stele*, as a similar monument close by is so called in its inscription. The traces of the religious paintings and monograms of this holy man still remain upon the backs of the marble of the bas-reliefs. I suggested a plan for withdrawing the sculpture from this monument, by building within the chamber a mass of stone-work close up to the cap-stone, in order to receive its weight when the marbles should be removed, then wedging up the cap-stone, on either side as the stones were withdrawn. This plan was condemned as unfeasible. For the Horse Tomb I proposed that sheers should be placed over it, and with blocks and ropes, or tightened cords afterwards wetted, the top should be raised and thus taken in pieces; but for this we had not the requisite machinery.

On the evening of Thursday, the 6th of January, Captain Graves, with eight gentlemen, among whom were Mr. Hoskyn and Lieutenant Spratt, two of his surveying officers, arrived in the course of a tour down the valley of the Xanthus, and proceeded on the morning of the 11th to make researches in the Cragus mountains. I regret that in this ramble of thirteen days in and around the Cragus mountains they did not find the ancient city of Cragus; they visited only Pinara, Cydna, and Sidyma.

Captain Graves spent the whole of Monday, the 10th, amidst the ruins, and I am glad that he witnessed the commencement of our discoveries. He saw the seven first stones which were found; upwards of seventy were afterwards discovered, but these he has never seen. I mentioned my plans for taking down the tombs to Mr. Hoskyn, but the Captain left orders that neither of them were to be touched, as we had not the requisite machinery. At Malta I had stated to the Admiral that flat-bottomed boats would be indispensable for removing the stones down the river : he replied, that if timber was to be had, the ship's carpenters would construct them. I mentioned this want to Captain Graves at Smyrna and at the mouth of the river. I now again urged the necessity for them, when he said that he would not have any of the stones taken down the river, and that proper stores must be obtained from Malta ; that he should bring his ship off the mouth of the river on the 1st of March to take all hands away. I urged that he should sail at once, or communicate by the post to the Admiral requesting more assistance ; but he replied that he would write to Captain Beaufort to know if he should proceed with this duty or go on with the survey, and that the answer could not be at Malta until March. I represented the loss of the season, and my necessary return to England before the completion of the expedition ; but the order was given, and the Captain, with both of his surveying officers, continued their tour on the morning of the 11th of January. A young assistant-surgeon who came with the party remained with us.

I took a solitary walk of some hours before I could decide upon my course of action. I need not say that I was annoyed. Before me lay a mine of treasure just opened, and all, whatever the extent, at our disposal ; I had an excellent set of willing working men, the best season in the year, ample authority from our own as well as the government of the Sultan, and no difficulties or wants but to communicate with Malta for the simple boats and machinery required. This was refused : whatever we found must be left behind until other ships were sent ; and, by the delay of our returning to Malta, the expedition would probably be too late for this season, on account of the heat of the weather and scarcity of water in the river. A year might pass over before the treasures would be safe in English custody ; ignorance of the peasantry, the curiosity or wantonness of travellers, might do them injury, or political changes might check the expedition.

I decided upon my plans. We had two carpenters who had hitherto worked with the men, these I employed solely in constructing crates and cases for securing the stones as soon as they were found ; but within ten days we discovered so many, that half of the men were obliged to work at the boats in bringing up timber to keep the carpenters employed. The carpenters, from the 21st of January until the 1st of March, worked a day and a half each day, and three or four of the stones were left uncased when we came away. Had our men been kept together, and the protection of the stones not been required, I know not what might have been the extent of our success. Up to this period I had never given any orders to the men ; the carpenters now acted under my instructions. The gunner, each morning at about nine o'clock, told me the orders he had received for the day, which ended about half-past four o'clock ; the hour for dinner divided the day.

On the 5th of January we saw from the heights above the city that the Isabella was off the coast, bringing us more men and some stores. Mr. Wilkinson was therefore sent down to see what assistance was required with camels or boats for the river. One of the Turks in the huts of Koonik lent him a horse, and about noon he trotted off down the valley. It was nearly six o'clock, and almost dark, when he returned with the sad news that a fatal accident had happened in landing the men on the beach. It appeared that the dingy, a small boat used for sending short distances ashore, had landed one load of stores and five men, and was again bringing a second. The sea being perfectly calm probably tempted them to overload the boat, for the boat had an anchor, a keg of spirits, and much baggage on board, besides seven men : she was consequently deep in the water ; a slight swell came on, and she was swamped. All went down within a hundred yards of the shore : two of the men who could not swim were lost. The most gallant spirit was shown by one of the survivors in returning to endeavour to rescue his companions, but they had sunk. The bodies of the men were afterwards washed on shore, and buried deep in the sand by their comrades. The cask of spirits alone swam to the shore, the weight of the anchor probably keeping the boat and her cargo at the bottom.

The report of the distress of the men, wet, cold, and

without the means of obtaining fire, as well as Wilkinson's haste to send them succour, caused him to lose his way amidst the high thickets : the horse's feet sank in the mud of the untracked road, and he became faint Wilkinson seeing the distant lights of our tents, dismounted, leaving his exhausted horse, and walked home with the sad news. He said that he knew where he had left the horse, and the next morning sent a Turk to seek it ; but the search was in vain. On the following day Wilkinson went himself, and found only the saddle, a part of the bridle, and one hoof ; the whole of the animal having been carried away and devoured by wolves. The marks of the blood and struggling of the horse pointed out the scene of its destruction.

Our researches amongst the ruins of the fallen temples continued to be successful. On the north side of the foundations, upon the cliff, after throwing over the heavy stones, three pieces of sculptured frieze lay in succession ; beneath these, other fragments of statues, and working downwards we found that we were within a cistern ten feet six inches long and six feet wide. This had been arched over, and an earthen pipe for conveying water was inserted at the corner : the cement with which it was lined still remained sound and perfectly smooth. As we proceeded to empty this cistern we found several heads of statues, architectural fragments, marble tiles and ridge-stones, and within a foot of the bottom a few inches of earth, beneath which lay the fragments of the top of the cistern. These had fallen with such force upon the cement at the bottom, that several stones had penetrated its surface, or the cistern would still have held water; the depth was six feet. On the opposite side, on the south, was a bank of earth and bushes, but I suspected that here also might be a cistern buried beneath. I therefore had the earth removed, and found another, containing portions of a frieze, and five or six lengths of fluted columns and cornices, several lions' faces forming waterspouts, and two statues—one a man with a child on his knee; together with numerous fragments of legs, arms and portions of broken sculpture. This cistern was circular, nine feet six inches in diameter, and the same in depth : earth and the fragments of the arched top filled the bottom of this also.

On the east of the foundation, being the side facing the level ground and opposite to the cliff, I found four pieces of frieze and a key-stone of the cornice, or border of a pediment : on the apex of this was a square cutting to receive a statue. Another piece of this cornice, forming one of the extreme angles, was also cut to receive a statue, about nine inches distant from the end. These made me hope to discover some statues ; and on the following day we dug up two figures lying close together, and one a few feet apart : these were of about the same scale, and had probably surmounted the pediment of a temple. Each of these statues displayed the emblems of Venus beneath their feet : one had a dove, another a dolphin, and the third a tortoise. The pleasure and excitement of these discoveries were entered

into even by the sailors, who often forgot the dinner
hour or worked after dusk to finish the getting out of a
statue : indeed, great care was needed to prevent their
being in too much haste to raise up the figures, for while
the marble was saturated with the moisture of the earth,
the slightest blow chipped off the light folds of the dra-
pery ; these hardened as they dried in the air. Beneath
the statues was a layer of chips, as in a mason's yard,
and beneath these the black natural earth, which was
always our signal for ceasing to excavate. On this level
we often found bronze pins and a kind of packing-needle,
and three or four small copper coins, which on examina-
tion proved to be the coins of the ancient Greek city.
In removing the large stones forming the avalanche in
front of the precipice, on the west side, we found, I
think, between thirty and forty pieces of sculptured
frieze, making about 220 feet of frieze and eleven statues,
from the site of this basement.

I must observe, what I cannot at all explain, that
these sculptures, from their various sizes and subjects,
must have formed four distinct friezes, and each of them
external, as the angles are sculptured. These stones I
found pell-mell one over the other ; and yet from the
metal ties remaining upon or near many of them, and
the fragments of heads or arms broken off in their fall
still lying close to the stone from which they had been
separated, I feel sure that all are as when first shaken
down by an earthquake.

Our depôt for stones, as soon as cased, was at the foot

of the cliff near which so many were found : this, therefore, was the constant haunt of our carpenters and men.
The sailors observed that two or three days in each week
a party of three or four Turks on horses, preceded by
ten or twelve fierce-looking hounds, passed by them
into the woods ; a Turk generally came before the dogs
making signs to the men to keep out of the way, as the
dogs were fierce : in an hour or two they returned, the
hounds looking much more docile, not requiring the
caution of the keeper. This mystery was explained the
following Sunday ; some of the sailors followed the
party, and found that the excursion was merely to feed
the dogs : often within a mile of the ruins they shot
two or three wild boars, which the dogs devoured, while
their masters dismounted to smoke their pipes. This
done, they returned home satisfied. The sailors soon
made known by signs that they would like to have a boar,
and through the interpreter their request was acceded to ;
but the Turks asked where their dogs were, not con-
ceiving it possible that any but dogs ever ate the unclean meat : no Mahometan will even touch the animal
or its skin. On the following day a fine boar was shot
for the men three miles from our quarters : the Turks
would not allow any of their horses to carry the dead
boar ; the sailors, therefore, with poles and hand-bar-
rows, brought home the huge beast. Sheers were soon
formed, and the boar suspended and cut up in a manner
worthy of an English butcher. All the Turks slunk off
one by one, for the first time disgusted with our manners.

I observed that they kept aloof for several days afterwards, and would never again accept of any of our food, even pudding or cake, fearing that we should mix up the unclean meat. The porcupine, which was one of our most delicious foods, was also offensive to them ; but they afterwards, on each hunting excursion, reported to our interpreter that they had shot and left for us to fetch away various animals. One day two bears were reported to be left, but my Greek cook here had his prejudices, although he made no allowance for the religious scruples of the Turks.

I have mentioned in my Journals of 1838 and 1840, the sculptures built into the walls of the ancient Acropolis, and have in them given representations of many. To remove these was our next object. The wall had been put together by the Romans, and is wholly composed of the ruins of some extremely ancient ornamented building, which most probably stood near the present site of the wall. On the other side of the Acropolis a similar wall is formed, running across the arc of the theatre. This is chiefly composed of the seats and ornamented chairs which formed the upper circles and places of honour in the theatre. The whole of the architecture, sculpture and inscriptions found upon the Acropolis and on its monuments in the rear, are of early Eastern character, and distinct from the Greek, which is the only style of art found in the other parts of the ruins in which we had been working. Eleven stones were lowered by means of long ropes (hawsers) down the almost perpendicular rock of the Acropolis, a height of about two hundred feet. Two statues of this early sculpture were also found imbedded or grouted into the centre of the wall with cement. The whole of these sculptures are of a school hitherto unknown in European museums.

By the 22nd of January so many stones were collected that I thought it prudent to secure what we had, and half the men went off with the boats for timber ; one assisted in sawing, and the seven that remained were employed in partial excavations where united force was unnecessary.

On the 26th of January Captain Graves sent Mr. Hoskyn from Macry to examine the river, and to report to him the best mode of transporting the stones to the coast. About this time I wrote the following letter to the Captain—

" Xanthus, 30th January, 1842.

" DEAR GRAVES,—Mr. Hoskyn arrived here on the 26th instant. I much regret that he or some capable officer was not sent sooner than a month after our arrival. Had our wants been ascertained by him at that time, or when I suggested them to you on the 10th of January, communication might have been made with Malta, and the expedition need not have been postponed to another season. I am sorry for the continued expenses of our Cavasses, &c., as we are all unoccupied here, carpenters alone being able to work at casing the marbles. Our work of discovering and removing the objects for casing commenced on the 10th and ended on the 21st instant, all hands at work ; since that time, of course, nothing has been done by the men, nor will there be above a day or two's work before we leave, although I think it probable the carpenters will not be able to finish by the 1st of March, the time you fixed for the Beacon to leave Macry. I again send a messenger for nails, who had better wait for one or two thousand, which I hear can be made in a day by the blacksmiths at Macry; but most probably you may have had some made, as the few (300) sent were not a day's supply. The Isabella not having been able to land her goods during the last ten days, we have also been without wood, but hope to begin work again as soon as the weather is more fine."

As it was tantalizing to seek about for objects which we should not be able to dig out or remove, I now confined myself for some time to re-copying, collating and taking impress casts on paper of the whole of the inscriptions in the Lycian language on the stele noticed in my former Journals *. From this position I had a view, at a short distance, of the Harpy Tomb, and was amused to see that the men under the Lieutenant were busily employed in constructing a tower within it, precisely as I had suggested, a plan which had been deemed unfeasible : I had not heard a word spoken on the subject since the Captain left orders that neither it nor the Horse Tomb should be touched. I never interfered with the undertaking, and only visited the spot when the men had left their work. The whole of the stones in four days were at our depôt for casing.

* This inscription will appear in the forthcoming volume of the Transactions of the Royal Society of Literature.

I must relate an anecdote in order to show how justice is here administered among the people, and their feeling toward us, a party sanctioned by the government. Ten stones were removed from the district of the Harpy Tomb on the sledge drawn by twenty men, making ten journeys across nearly a quarter of a mile of growing corn, then about two or three inches above the ground. This damage could not be avoided by us, but as soon as we had finished, I had the fences restored, and sent to the owner to request that he would state the injury done, that I might repay him. He said that he would call the head men of the neighbouring villages together and they should decide. On the following Friday (their Sunday) a party of eight or nine Turks walked thoughtfully over the land, stooping and examining the corn ; in the course of an hour they gave their report, that " trampling the corn down and the cutting off the blade with the sledge had not destroyed the seed, and that if God sent rain it would spring up again, and that no damage was done." I was sorry for this decision, as I did not wish to have it said that we had not repaid them something ; I therefore drew their attention to the furrow ploughed up by dragging a stick of timber over the ground ; after reconsideration they assessed this damage at five piastres, about thirteen pence. I paid the owner three times that amount, and all were satisfied.

The gunner informed me one morning at half-past eight o'clock, that they were going to pull down the Horse Tomb. I begged that he would delay for an hour, as I wished to mark with lines and numbers the various cracks and stones upon the middle story, and to map them accurately, as I felt sure it would fall in pieces as soon as the weight of the top was removed. This I did, and left the men to proceed with this monument also, for the removal of which I had suggested plans, differing altogether from those now adopted. My feelings were the same as with respect to the Harpy Tomb, and I did not interfere, except to request them to clear away previously all stones from around, and afterwards to preserve any fragment which might fall. The means adopted appeared to me to be more sailor-like than scientific: the men placed slings and cords over the top, which probably weighed ten tons, and making blocks fast to the neighbouring rocks, *hauled* the top off. As I anticipated, the centre fell in pieces, but the sculptured parts did not receive more injury than they probably would have done from a more scientific operation. The whole may be easily restored, and will again form one of the most elegant and interesting monuments I have ever seen. The several parts of this tomb are so heavy that it is necessary they should be cut : I have therefore marked with black paint the lines for the saw, in order that the sculpture should not be injured. This will reduce the weight of the various parts so that they may be packed in cases ; I also did this with the tomb, with lions resembling the Persepolitan sculpture.

Some of the men formed a party, taking with them port-fires, to explore some arched vaults running beneath

a huge pile of building attributable to the Greek age :
after proceeding about thirty yards, other passages
branched off, forming the crypt, or substructure of the
halls above; all these were dry and in good preser-
vation. A Turkish short sword inlaid with silver, a
flask made of a small gourd and half filled with gunpowder, a pocket pistol with flint lock, much braiding
and silk buttons, fragments of a black silk handkerchief
marked with blood, and the lower jaw-bone of a man
containing all the teeth sound, were found in one of
those passages. The jaw-bone, the only trace of the
owner of these treasures, was judged by our surgeon to
have been that of a negro. The pistol * was loaded with
ball, and the powder retained all its igneous properties.
There can be little doubt that wild beasts had dragged
the probably dead man into this their den, leaving only
those things, which, had it been the work of a robber,
would have been taken away. We may infer from the
sheathed sword and loaded pistol that the man had not
been called upon to defend himself, and that he had not
been murdered for the sake of his property. An iron
spike with wooden handle, similar to an instrument I
have seen used by the Turks in agriculture, was also
found near the same place.

* On removing the rust from the pistol, which was of very common
manufacture, the name of Dover was found upon the lock. I find that
a salesman of cheap fire-arms of that name lived in London about sixty
years ago, which may give an idea of the date.

Provisions are here very cheap. Oxen or sheep were killed and weighed to us at one piastre per oke, being 1¼ lb. for a penny : wheaten bread made for us was the same price, but we paid the carriage of it from Fornas, eight miles distant : the finest oranges from Rhodes were one para each, equal to seventeen for a penny : woodcocks, wild-ducks and partridges were very abundant. Mahomet, a youth of eighteen, the son of our landlady, received each week the amount of our rent, which was generally acknowledged by presents of cream, fruit or game. I asked what his mother would do with the money we had paid to her, and suggested that they should increase their stock of cattle ; but he said, why should they ? they had enough. I then proposed that they should cultivate more land for corn. His reply was to the same effect, " their stock of corn always lasted until the return of the harvest." He then said that the money would make a dowry for his sisters. At our departure his mother was in tears, when she confessed that at first she was afraid of us, but she now found that Franks were quite as good as Turks, and hoped we should come to the country again. We kept on admirable terms with the peasantry, and I believe our departure was a subject of regret to all. Our English spades, pickaxes and tools were much admired and often borrowed by the people, but always punctually returned*.

* At my request the tools, when the expedition was concluded, were given to the Aga to distribute among the peasantry.

One of the prettiest sights I witnessed while at Xanthus was caused by the novelty and use of our carpenter's grindstone ; the peasantry came down from miles around to sharpen their tools. This became troublesome to our workmen, and the handle was taken off. The use of the stone then became a favour, which I often granted in order to oblige them, and to see the groups assembled around ; each had his sword, pruning-hook, axe, knife or ploughshare in his hand, and patiently awaited his turn at the stone. On leaving the country I promised the people that I would send them one, to be placed under the care of young Mahomet, for the use of all the peasantry of the valley ; and I hear from Malta that my present was sent and highly appreciated. I have never seen gritstone in that district of Asia Minor, and the native limestone rocks are a poor substitute for the revolving stone which they now possess.

While at Xanthus I had several European visitors. Professor Schönbrun of Posen, one of five learned Prussians who, at the instigation of their government or universities, are carrying out the investigations of this country, remained with me two days : at my suggestion he kindly examined several points : he discovered that the monument seen by me only at a distance, to the north of Cadyanda, had been inscribed in the Lycian character, but was rendered illegible by decay. He traced an ancient wall cutting across the valley, about six miles above the city of Xanthus : this is highly interesting, as it no doubt perfected the natural division of the countries of the early inhabitants, the Troes and Tramelæ, the former, which was the kingdom of Pandarus, having Tlos and Pinara for its chief cities. The ruins at the north-east end of the valley of Cassabar he found to be those of the small Greek city of Arna ; those near the coast at Kakava, the city of Cyanæ. The city of Caunus he had previously identified, on the straits connecting the bay or lake of Koojez with the sea : this is in Caria. The Rev. Mr. Daniell often came from the ship, making my hut his home while visiting and sketching the neighbouring Lycian cities. He discovered two inscriptions in the ruins at Horahn, which I suggested might be found to be the ancient Massicytus, giving it the name of Araxa. I had also visits from Mr. Edward Forbes, the well-known naturalist, who had been for the past year in Lycia, and Mr. Sanford, an English gentleman, whose residence at Rhodes had been prolonged for nearly a twelvemonth, solely attracted by the kindness and excellence of the Turkish character. He had been studying the Turkish language and endeavouring to repay the kindness of the people by suggesting improvements in their agriculture, and introducing to them potatoes and other seeds. He speaks highly of the literary and well-informed society of the leading people among the Turks.

I shall avoid giving any description of the sculptures, which ere long will be better judged of in the British Museum, but I shall recapitulate their localities. On the Acropolis, which must have formed the city of the

earliest inhabitants, were found all the works of a pecu-
liar eastern character,—the works of the Troes and of the
Tramelæ. The cemeteries of these peoples are marked
as theirs, by their formation, by being generally cut in
the rock, by their sculpture, and the characters of the
inscriptions; these tombs are principally in the rocky
cliffs to the south-east. The city, built in the manner
of the Greeks, seems to have been added to that of the
early people, but its style of building does not appear
to have extended over the old Acropolis. In this Greek-
built district the sculpture and inscriptions are Greek;
and, from the subjects of the bas-reliefs, the place must
have contained buildings with friezes, representing the
capture of the early city—so accurately illustrating the
description given in Herodotus, that I could almost fancy
that the neighbouring historian had written his history
from this frieze, commemorating an event which happened about a century before his æra. The cemeteries of
this people are very extensive, spreading for two miles to-
wards the south-east of the city, and also on the western
side of the river. All these are sarcophagi, bearing Greek
inscriptions. These cities, we read*, were conquered by
Brutus, and the description of the capture is fully borne
out by the present position of the walls. The Roman
conqueror appears to have destroyed most of the buildings
of the city, which must have been crowded with temples
and public edifices. The materials of these, with reversed
capitals, cornices, inscriptions and even statues, now form

* Plutarch's Life of Brutus.

walls of fortification to all the surrounding heights, and mostly built with cement : these range over an extent of some miles in circuit. I have found no Roman tombs or inscriptions, nor have I seen any sculpture or art of that people, excepting the piling together of walls.

The next conquest appears to have been the effort of nature ; evident marks of destruction and disjointing by the shocks of earthquakes are visible. This was probably eitherat the period of the destruction of the Colossus of Rhodes (B.C. 214), or at the time mentioned by Tacitus (A.D. 17), since which period I see no reason to believe that any but a solitary hermit has inhabited this city. A Turkish khan, probably used half a century ago, has been constructed amidst the ruins : it has fallen to decay, and the present inhabitants of the district live in huts and tents scattered around, but not amidst the ruins of the ancient city.

At the latter end of February we were making preparations for removing to the coast, to await the arrival of the ship on the 1st of March. My great care was the finishing the cases, which were now very nearly completed. I proposed leaving them in charge of the Aga of Fornas until the arrival of some English ship, and therefore numbered and marked each case, corresponding with my descriptive catalogue : I also made two lists, showing the position of the 82 cases, one for the Aga, and the other for the Pasha at Rhodes. I sent to the Aga the following request ; that he should take charge of the cases, and employ such guard as he saw fit, and that I would pay him any expenses incurred. After every mark of friendly reception of my message, and due consideration, he declined taking them under his charge, saying, that if it was a hundred or a thousand pounds he would take charge of it, because if lost he could replace it, or, if injured by the people, he would tax them to restore the amount,—but how could he replace such stones as those ? His reasoning was too simple and powerful for me to urge him further. I gave the list to the Pasha at Rhodes, who sent two men over to protect them, but only held himself responsible for the conduct of the men, not for the safety of the marbles. We are so accustomed to receive equivalents in insurance, that we feel no scruples in holding ourselves responsible for almost anything.

Early on the morning of the 3rd of March we were all on board the Beacon ship, and arrived at Rhodes on the 5th. A few hours sufficed for all we had to do with the authorities, and we sailed on for Malta. I received letters at Rhodes from the Trustees of the British Museum, very handsomely acknowledging my services in obtaining the firman from Constantinople, and sanctioning any expenses I might have incurred on that occasion.

On the 14th of March we arrived at Malta, bearing the Captain's report to the Admiral : had this been sent two months before, we might by this time have been there with all the stones on board, or, by remaining a month later, have in all probability found double the number of treasures.

I received every possible attention from the authorities at Malta. Admiral Sir Thomas Mason, commander-in-chief, Admiral Sir John Lewis, and Major Yule of the Engineers, almost daily called upon or corresponded with me in lazaretto, obtaining all the information I could give to forward a fresh expedition to bring away the cases. I was applied to for the accurate measurement of each stone, in order that the officers of Engineers should calculate the weight : the result of which was, that the 82 cases together weighed 80 tons, the three largest stones weighing 2 tons 1 cwt. each.

Admiral Sir Edward Owen arrived to take the chief command on the 4th of April, and immediately requested an interview with Captain Graves and myself; when the Admiral said to Captain Graves, " I understand that it is your wish to leave this duty and continue your survey ;" the Captain replied, " It is, Sir ; " thus voluntarily giving up the expedition into the hands of others.

Having done all I could in instructing the officers about to be employed, I left Malta on the 6th of April for Marseilles in the French steam-packet. Before leaving I understood that the expedition would start in two or three days. I urged the necessity, in my letter to the Admiral, as well as verbally, that no time should be lost ; as the season, from my experience of the climate, would be too hot, and that I feared if the expedition were there after the middle of May the waters from the melting snows would have ceased to fill the river, which would probably become too shallow for navigation. I regret to say that the Medea steam-ship, appointed for the service, did not leave Malta until the 28th of April, and then sailed to Athens, not arriving at Xanthus until the 13th of May, the time at which all the work should have been accomplished. It was the 8th of June before the party left the coast. At this season the Turks had put the valley under irrigation, and had themselves retired to their summer farms in the Yeeilassies of the mountains. Noctious evaporation and malaria were the consequence, and fever appeared among the seamen on board the Monarch at anchor off the coast. The stone sawyers taken from Malta to divide the heavy stones of the Horse Tomb had several weeks' work before them; it was impossible to allow the sailors to remain in the country, therefore all sailed away, bringing 78 of the cases and leaving the Horse Tomb for another season. The striking beauty of this monument will be the guarantee for its arriving where art is appreciated.

The 78 cases were safely deposited at Malta by the end of June, and were brought to England in H.M. ship Cambridge in December.

I cannot close this account without adding the very flattering resolution of the Trustees of the British Museum, passed May 14, soon after my arrival in England.

"May 14th, 1842.

" *His Grace the Archbishop of Canterbury in the Chair.*

[After ordering the repayment of the sums which I advanced] It was resolved :—

"That the Trustees desire to express their sense of Mr. Fellows's public spirit, in voluntarily undertaking to lend to so distant an expedition the assistance of his local knowledge and personal co-operation; and that they have viewed with great satisfaction the decision and energy evinced by Mr. Fellows in proceeding from Smyrna to Constantinople and obtaining the necessary authority for the removal of the marbles, as well as his judicious directions at Xanthus, by which the most desirable of the valuable monuments of antiquity, formerly brought to light by him, together with several others of scarcely less interest now for the first time discovered and excavated, have been placed in safety, and, as the Trustees have every reason to hope, secured for the National Museum.

(Signed)   " J. FORSHALL, *Secretary*."

THE END.

Printed by Richard and John E. Taylor, Red Lion Court, Fleet Street.

www.ingramcontent.com/pod-product-compliance
Ingram Content Group UK Ltd.
Pitfield, Milton Keynes, MK11 3LW, UK
UKHW042150280225
455719UK00001B/231